STRENGTHENING SCHOOL—COMMUNITY RELATIONS

Strengthening
School-Community Relations

Robert Byrne
Edward Powell

National Association of Secondary School Principals
1904 Association Drive
Reston, Virginia 22091

Copyright 1976
National Association of Secondary School Principals

ISBN 0-88210-075-0

Foreword

How can an effective community relations program benefit the school? How, in fact, can the school administrator identify the school community? And—once identified—what is the most effective method of communication with that community?

In providing answers for these and other related questions, authors Robert Byrne and Edward Powell have relied on first-hand experience. As a result, this publication contains a wealth of practicable information for every principal. Whether the reader is a beginning administrator or one with significant experience the suggestions are on target.

We commend them to your full and serious consideration.

>Owen B. Kiernan
>Executive Secretary
>National Association of
> Secondary School Principals

Planning the Effort

When a man assumes a public trust, he should consider himself as public property.
—Thomas Jefferson

It is perhaps unfortunate that terms such as "community relations," "interaction," and "interface" have been added to that large, amorphous vocabulary that is loosely labeled "educationese." Educationese is a familiar demon to those of us in public education who have encountered glib leaders who substitute mind-boggling terminology for solid, workable ideas. Simply stated, it is jargon, a type of lingo just sophisticated enough to pass through and beyond the well-intentioned objections of those most closely associated with teaching.

Educationese is used nowhere more often than in the field of school-community relations. Every school administrator has heard the term, and many have hatched their own vague "affirmative action plans," adding more musty pages to the seldom-consulted tomes of administrative policy and procedure. Despite the fanfare, school-community relations for many parents has been limited to that sweltering June afternoon when they were forced to mass uncomfortably on a football field while a reluctant principal directed the standard commencement exercises in competition with the static of an aging microphone and horns from an adjacent highway.

In the 1970s "public relations" has become a watchword for the successful school administrator. But in too many school districts, "PR" is a substitute for rather than a supplement to a productive program of community interaction. Public school salesmanship is, unhappily, a necessity in a society that has made a fad of debunking its own institutions.

The astute school administrator is normally quick to realize that, in the final analysis, he is his own best advocate. Obviously, as a leader in the school, he is familiar with the school's accomplishments; but more importantly, even the most glittering successes will go unheralded if they are not enthusiastically explained for parents and the press.

However, it is the one-sidedness of many modern public relations efforts that can spell their own doom. Too many interested observers of the public education scene have for too long been hoodwinked by an endless stream of success stories that have belied the reality of struggle, conflict, and failure in the schools. Honesty, candor, and plain talk rather than the convoluted language of quasi-professionals are the key aspects of long-term success in the public relations program. One side of the story is not enough. "Tell them the truth," stated one official, "first, because it is right and second, because they'll find out anyway."

Essentials of a Sound Communications Program

There is no way to effectively prepare a "cookbook" on human relations; we can't stir some ingredients in a pot and come up with a batch of congeniality. The human factor in human relations is just too elusive and unpredictable for the simplistic methods of the technicrat. Nevertheless, the rudiments of a sound community relations program can be delineated and discussed. It should be emphasized, however, that the essentials of the program do not guarantee success. They are merely the elements without which success can never be achieved.

Community relations involves a planned effort.

Interaction with the public is going to occur whether or not school administrators approve of it or care about it. The administrator's task is to predict the direction of this interaction, possibly chart its course, and ensure that it has a salutary effect on the school system. The current communications procedure within the system must be diagnosed before the overall strategy for change can be developed.

Community relations involves common sense, but hopefully it is much more than that. The time for community relations planning is not when the dissidents are hammering on the principal's door. The community relations plan must be formulated using recognizable goals that are suitably individualized for each school district. Responsibilities must be defined; implementation of the plan must be energetic, not half-hearted and passive; the plan must be evaluated objectively and changed as necessary.

Community relations involves everyone in the educational system.

The community relations program cannot begin and end with the ambitious guidance counselor or assistant principal who concocts patchwork information programs in relative isolation from the remainder of the school population. Of course, ambitious and enthusiastic professionals can be important contributors to the plan and the program, but their efforts must be integrated with the district plan for communications.

The degree of staff involvement can be expected to vary. There are some individuals who are simply uncomfortable in the presence of any kind of organizational change. However, everyone should be involved according to his interests and talents and no one should be uninvolved or uninformed.

Community relations includes involvement as well as information.

If there was ever a truism in school public relations, it is that citizens know less about their schools than educators think they do. What little they do know is derived mainly from their own children.

Although some degree of salesmanship is necessary in the public school, it must include more than "sales talk" and go beyond a recitation of management accomplishments. Sharing in school information is a prelude to a deeper quality of involvement. "Interaction" implies an "action" role for the community in problem solving, data gathering, and the decision-making process. Involvement, rather than information, is the key to development of good school-community relations.

The community relations program must support innovation and creativity.

The encouragement of creativity will usually result in diversity and challenges to tradition and conformity. Occasionally, these challenges will be inconvenient to the pursuit of other goals. The administrator and his staff cannot afford to disdain well-intentioned, thoughtful criticism of existing policies and procedures. Indeed, sensitivity to community input necessitates careful consideration of ideas and a change of plan when necessary.

When discussing the "self-renewing" organization, John W. Gardner stated that "men cannot be prisoners of procedures." An innovative organization needs structures for self-criticism. Singular reliance on the dictates and whims of management will ensure failure for any organization. A school administrator is no more vulnerable than when he is sheltered by well-meaning but spineless subordinates who hang on the chief's words and avoid the risk of their own recommendations.

The community relations program must be accompanied by a commitment of time, resources, and personnel.

As do the suggestion boxes that are never emptied, tall-order missions that are short on the methods and means of accomplishment endanger staff morale. Leadership in community relations may or may not be synonymous with leadership in other spheres of school management. Leadership ability among teachers and parents may surface, and should be nurtured. Communication consultants can be drafted from other districts or from universities. In any event, the administrator must ensure that the right personnel are directing the communications effort.

Similarly, sufficient time to accomplish the necessary tasks is essential. Staff cannot be expected to meet on their own time or to leave classrooms and schools unsupervised. The community relations objectives must be served by adequate resources, and time and personnel are critical among them.

The community relations program must provide for appropriate evaluation procedures.

Feedback should be sought at each step in the community relations process. Educators and parents should continuously examine their progress and take stock of their actions in view of their objectives. Surveys may be a good source of feedback, and can indicate directions for change.

The community relations program must reach the community power structure.

Neither the community nor its school system escapes political realities. What has been termed the community "power puzzle" must be clearly understood by the administrator and his staff. A power structure, both formal and informal, exists within every community. The various members of this power structure usually have fairly well-formed notions of what they feel the public school should be, and will exert conflicting demands upon the school system.

Understanding the community power structure does not imply that school policy should be conditioned to accord with community sanctions. Schools exist to serve children equally, despite their parents' backgrounds or inclinations to speak up at the school board meeting. Nevertheless, the power structure usually holds the key to issues and problems for which community relations must account.

Obstacles to Effective Community Relations

In view of the almost compelling need for school community interactions, one wonders why more concerted, positive action has not been taken. Some common reasons follow.

Reluctance among administrators.

Despite broad education in psychology, curriculum, and social science the typical school administrator's background is largely in the realm of research and theory. Rarely do graduate courses provide for practical application. Only recently have graduate schools instituted administrative internships, and even now they are not required for administrative certification in many states. The wide spectrum of interpersonal skills ranging from public speaking to group dynamics is often completely excluded from graduate education programs, even at the doctoral level. Consequently, a young professional administrator is forced to learn by doing in a new and high-pressure environment.

The neophyte administrator soon learns that life in the trenches is fraught with difficulties. The overwhelming demands of staff, students, and curriculum often combine to make the administrator a reactive rather than a proactive agent in the organizational hierarchy. Add to this a host of weekly unanticipated calamities such as a riot in the cafeteria, an unexpected staff resignation, or a custodians' job action and there is precious little time to interact with one's own spouse, let alone the community at large. School administration in the '70s has placed ever-increasing responsibilities on educational leaders.

A deeper and more serious obstacle to risking an active program of community interaction among administrative personnel is "failure shock," the belief that "if anything can go wrong, it will." This condition is intensified by the plethora of trained administrators, the unwavering demand for excellence in middle management, and the fierce determination to survive when real achievement is either unattainable or unmeasurable. Administrators, committed to the avoidance of errors, often miss their chance for success. At the extreme, all administrative decisions are considered in terms of how failure might be penalized and how it can be explained away once it occurs.

Failure shock symptoms partially explain the cautious approach to community interaction endeavors. On a more critical level, they explain a good deal of the inertia that has existed in public schools over the past two decades.

Resistance in the teaching staff.

Although many teachers will welcome an administrator's effort to embark on a community relations program, there will almost always exist a hard core of detractors who will oppose any kind of organizational change. The varied sources of this resistance have been the subject of considerable speculation on the part of social science theorists. On one level the reason may involve an implied or direct threat to job, status, or vested interests and security of individuals accustomed to a predictable organizational climate. The reason also may be an honest conviction that the change is wrong, or a lack of confidence in the person or persons who are initiating the change.

In situations where administrator-staff relationships are strained over other matters, the condition is far more difficult. Goodwin Watson described the illusion of staff impotence as a "we-they" attitude.[1] In the minds of a cowed staff, all problems are attributable to that vague, undefined authority figure known as "them." "They" got us into this mess and "they" can devise a way out. Feeling trapped and helpless, the staff will assume no responsibility and very little initiative.

Watson offers suggestions for reducing the inevitable resistance. The project should clearly have the enthusiastic support of top management officials; it should offer a new and interesting experience without threatening autonomy and security in any manner; the staff

---

1. Goodwin Watson, ed., *Concepts for Social Change* (Washington, D.C.: NTL Institute for Applied Behavioral Science, National Education Association, 1967) p. 18.

should see the project as a product of its own efforts; and in the long run it should be viewed as reducing rather than increasing present burdens. The organizational aim of the administrator is a type of "change readiness" that necessitates broad staff involvement and an authorized structure for the resisters to express their opinions.

Criticism from the social milieu.

In any community there are an astounding number of self-made critics who do not hesitate to express considerable disagreement as to what children should learn and even why and how they should learn.

A budding school-community relations program soon finds itself needing public cooperation on the one hand and facing inevitable conflict on the other. When not handled with cautious diplomacy, the program can create more problems than it solves.

Community Relations and Sound Educational Management

Much has been written regarding community expectations of the public school. Schools, in turn, have made considerable demands upon a relatively uninformed society for financial, moral, and in some cases volunteer support. If schools are really "public," then the public has a stake not only in their current achievement, but in their future development as well.

The development of an effective community relations program should be viewed as nothing less than sound and essential educational management. Community relations is the school administrator's medium for the expression of critical educational needs. It is an opportunity for face-to-face contact with an often concealed but significant part of his clientele. It is a source for new ideas and the best chance for furthering the growth and development of a vital social institution.

In his often-cited proposition for educational transition, Daniel Griffiths stated that "the degree and duration of change is directly proportional to the intensity of the stimulus from the supra system." He indicates that solid educational transition will occur only when the system is willing to stray beyond its own boundaries.[2]

Active community interaction programs are risky business. Interaction involves change, and change brings on conflict. Leaders are wary of conflicts because in a conflict situation, the needs of one individual are sometimes realized at the expense of another. However, community interaction is worth the risk. In fact, it is not a question of whether the system can afford expensive public communication. In a time of stress and decision, it is more a question of when and how the communication effort can be initiated.

---

2. Daniel Griffiths. "Administrative Theory and Change in Organization," in *Organization and Human Behavior*, ed. Fred Carner and Thomas Sergiovanni (New York: Mc Graw Hill, 1969) pp. 370-371.

Preparing the Staff and the Students

Lord, reform thy world, beginning with me.
—*Prayer of a Chinese Christian, quoted by President Franklin D. Roosevelt in a press conference, December 17, 1941.*

Many administrators are hampered in staff and student communication by a lack of awareness, by a lack of communications format or plan, and by a tendency to get tied down with details and routines. Staff cooperation is essential to the community communications effort. Without such cooperation, the administrator's "overtures to the public" will appear to be one-sided and superficial, rather than part of an organized system. In short, the school must have solid and healthy internal communications if community relations objectives are to be achieved.

Behavioral and administrative science literature is replete with experiments and studies dealing with "climate" in social organizations. For our purpose, organizational climate is defined as the quality of the relationship between superior and subordinate. Organizational climate will be positive when the staff members feel secure and when they recognize a genuine interest in their welfare. There is a general feeling that their actions will be considered objectively and impartially and that in any given instance, they will "get a fair break." Administrative initiatives that contribute to a positive organizational climate include a complete and continuous information program and a commitment to involve staff in the important issues, decisions, and problems that confront the school or school district.

Informing the Staff

Personal communication.

Undoubtedly, the administrator's most effective method in communicating with teachers is through personal contact. Unfortunately, this time-consuming method is the least efficient. Although personal contact should be sought whenever possible, other communications media will often have to be utilized.

Memos and bulletins.

In most schools, memos and bulletins are used too often. The more often they are issued, the less impact they are likely to have. A general staff information bulletin, published weekly, is preferable to an avalanche of memos from administrators, counselors, and instructional supervisors. The memo is best suited for information that can't wait for a meeting or the weekly bulletin.

Faculty liaison committee.

In larger schools and school districts, the liaison committee can be a crucial structure for information dissemination. Its use provides the advantages of personal contact and economy of time. More importantly, because it is outside the organizational hierarchy, the liaison group can be a powerful and persuasive force.

Open door policy.

Teachers should be provided immediate assistance and advice when required. Advice and assistance should be available from any administrator to whom the teacher directs his problem. Firsthand counseling underscores individual security and demonstrates that direct and personal consideration is available, despite the structure and size of the school.

Open door policies run the risk of breeding suspicion among lower-level supervisors who may feel they are being bypassed. Therefore, conferences must be conducted diplomatically. As a general rule, the open door policy should not be used for leverage against other administrators or a teacher's colleagues. No one in the system is suitably served by gossip and reprisals.

Auxiliary personnel.

Auxiliary personnel have a marked influence on students and their parents. In this category is the bus driver, whose daily contact with students is almost as extensive as a teacher's; the school custodian, who consistently interacts with students in classrooms and in the hallways both during and after school; and the school secretary, who is constantly arranging student appointments, planning meetings, and conversing with parents on the telephone.

Although custodians do not have the same information needs as teachers, there may be aspects of school policy that should reach custodians and all other school employees. It may very well be a custodian's or secretary's good judgment or blunder that affects the attitudes of a student and his parents.

Building Staff Involvement

Shared decision making is often misunderstood as an abdication of administrative authority. There is an understandable and palpable fear that sharing responsibility will frustrate the decision-making machinery and make the system vulnerable to the "fringe" thinking of the more vocal and extreme elements of the faculty.

What is missed in the general confusion on this matter is that the decision-making process involves elements other than the mere rendering of the decision. And in many respects, problem identification, the generation and selection of alternatives, and the prediction of consequences, are more challenging and time consuming than the dispensing of decisions once the groundwork has been completed.

Staff involvement in policy formation and decision making has advantages that outweigh the risks:

- Staff members can provide input that is realistic and practical and often suggest ideas that may be overlooked by higher level management.
- Staff morale may improve when ideas that originate with the staff are translated into district policy.
- Staff involvement will strengthen the organizational structure, and thereby make events, policies, and practices more predictable.

The principal mechanism for involving staff is the workshop or staff committee. In workshops, teachers can rely upon their own experiences to assist others in identifying problems and searching for solutions. An effective use of the staff workshop would be the development of a plan for community relations and interaction. Teachers and administrators could collaborate on role definitions, program objectives, extent of involvement, and perhaps some innovative community projects.

Some other committee activities which might be conducted concurrently with the community relations workshop are listed below:

- Ongoing study and selection of instructional resources such as books, tapes, films, and other instructional materials for inclusion in the curriculum.
- Delineating and formalizing job expectations and preparing position guides.
- Sharing effective approaches to student discipline.
- Exploring student rights and responsibilities.
- Assessing and suggesting ways to improve the teacher evaluation system.
- Reviewing and revising the scope and sequence of learning activities, suggesting new courses that coincide with faculty interests and strengths.
- Investigating new approaches to grading and reporting, resolving controversies on the use and misuse of grades.
- Reviewing procedures and suggesting ways to deal with student absenteeism.

- Sharing effective ways of improving classroom technique, suggesting resources for purchase.
- Working with state and national associations to plan for teacher attendance and participation at conferences, suggesting standards of financial remuneration.
- Recommending and assessing extracurricular activities.

The specific composition of the workshops is less critical than the common ground that exists throughout their structure: administrators and teachers working together toward common goals and the interdependency of both groups. Enthusiasm and motivation to continue the committees will be self-sustaining as long as committee recommendations are considered and adopted.

Involving the Students

In one of his more delightful observations upon adolescence, Mark Twain stated: "When I was a boy of fourteen, my father was so ignorant I could hardly stand to have the old man around. But when I was twenty-one I was astonished at how much the old fellow had learned in seven years."

There are those of conservative leaning who state with conviction and not a little bit of sense that "students come to school to learn." Notwithstanding the urging of traditionalist colleagues (and the suggestion of author Twain), students both desire and deserve a voice in planning and shaping the education that will have an overwhelming effect on the direction and pattern of their lives.

Administrators who demur at the suggestion of faculty involvement in educational decision making are likely to shudder at the prospects of student participation. Nevertheless, the rationale with respect to community relations is similar. The aims of the communications program require student understanding and student support.

Formal structures for communication with the student body have existed for many years in the secondary school. However, the reliance upon these structures for anything other than student opinions has rarely existed. Again, the important factor is not the structure but the quality of the interaction between administrators and students and the consideration of student ideas in reviewing and revising policy. Here are some suggestions for improving student involvement:
- A student curriculum council. The council meets on a recurring basis (perhaps every two weeks) to review matters pertaining to instruction and curriculum. Students discuss the relevance of instruction, suggest curricular trends, and perhaps survey the student population for ideas for future course development.
- A student school management council. This group advises the administration on all facets of school operations: rights and responsibilities, discipline codes, extra-curricular activities, and ways that students and staff can join forces to improve the school environment.
- A community activities committee. Students take an active role

in planning and preparing for all events involving the community. They act as hosts and, wherever possible, as speakers and chairpersons for activities.
- Assemblies. The oldest of student communication devices is still one of the most reliable. In large schools, assemblies should be scheduled often for pupils of a given grade, both for information and entertainment. Those preferring not to attend should be permitted to go to class, student cafeteria, or lounge.
- Homerooms. Homerooms provide an excellent opportunity for administrators and counselors to discuss problems in small groups. An information program through the homeroom is most effective when it is preplanned.
- Student publications. Publications should be encouraged and adequately funded. Student newspaper and yearbook staffs might work through local newspapers and journals in order to share and develop information. They should develop their own journalism guidelines, establish standards, and supervise their own ranks.

Conclusion

The commitment to community relations involves an unleashing of the communications potential within the school that extends to faculty, auxiliary personnel, and students. Effective interaction with the community must be accompanied by open communication in every segment of the school population. It must be an integral aspect of the organizational structure and must continuously focus on the school's problems.

Behind the communications structure are the workings of the administrators. Administrators organize, develop, and encourage the participation of students, teachers, and other school personnel.

Community Analysis

This is the final test of a gentleman: his respect for those who can be of no possible service to him.
—William L. Phelps

In the post-Watergate era, the phrase "political power" is often received with suspicion and fear. We have grown weary of power politics and scornful of a system that perpetuates privilege and "deals" that serve the interests of a selected few.

Nevertheless, at all levels of government and in large organizations, the reality of power persists. The question of whether power is desirable is almost irrelevant. The fact is that power in the form of social and organizational influence exists now and will continue to be a major factor in government and community.

Because we often tend to confuse the mere existence of power with its misuse, it is important that a working definition be stated. According to Floyd Hunter, power refers to the "acts of men going about the business of moving other men to act in relation to themselves or in relation to organic or inorganic things." The definition assumes that the influence of individuals is relatively limited when separated from organizations, formal groups, or associations.[1] It is with these organizational entities that the school executive must begin his study of community relationships and influence.

Purpose of Community Analysis

The school administrator needs to understand the educational philosophy of the community in order to determine whether the community approves or disapproves of the school program.[2] The com-

---

1. Floyd Hunter, *Community Power Structure* (Chapel Hill, N.C.: University of North Carolina Press, 1953).

2. Robert P. Bullock, *School-Community Attitude Analysis for Educational Administrators*, SCDS Monograph No. 7 (Columbus: The Ohio State University, 1959) p. 112.

munity's understanding of administrator and teacher roles as well as its receptivity to change and innovation also figure in community relations.

Of course, there are no clear-cut answers to the questions relating to community analysis. Robert Bullock discovered in one urban district that educational philosophy varied in terms of residence, occupation, organizational memberships, and the level of formal education.[3] The task of the administrator is to both understand the range of community attitudes and aspirations and to integrate them into a viable and acceptable program of action.

The understandable fear of many educators is that the school will become a pawn in the larger arena of community politics—in itself a strong argument for a community analysis program. Objective, impartial analysis of the various sources of community power will alert the school administrator to the possible effects of one organization's exerting a disproportionate influence on educational decisions.

Administrators have often been criticized for introducing politics into the workings of the schools. However, school administrators must understand the power status of the community if they are to act with reference to community standards and values. Involvement in the community becomes manipulation when administrative decisions abridge the rights and prerogatives of others. This is not to be confused with the school administrator's leadership function of assisting the community to reflect its values in formulating educational goals.

Basic Assumptions About Communities

The notion of a monolithic community power structure, although common, is erroneous. The decisions of school boards and administrations are affected by the external environment, but not in a uniform manner. In discussing the relationship between power and policy, Ralph Kimbrough stated that educational decision making occurs through the interaction of formally appointed or elected individuals with the unofficial interest groups that express the special needs of their constituents.[4]

The plurality of power concept is not inconsistent with the social scientist's understanding of the community as a "system of systems." A given community—municipal, suburban, rural, or any mix thereof—is composed of many different institutions and organizations with formal and informal subgroups. These groups and subgroups represent a diversity of needs, interests, goals, and activities.

Consequently, community power, unlike the power of a formal bureaucracy, is neither structurally nor functionally centralized. Among the variety of separate groups, it is rare that one group will maintain a completely dominant position. Of equal importance is the

---
3. Ibid., p. 112.
4. Ralph Kimbrough, *Political Power and Educational Decision Making* (Chicago: Rand McNally, 1964).

fact that the values, ideals, and ambitions of the community will reflect the range of subsystems within the community. Of course, patterns will emerge, but they will very often be nebulous and difficult to isolate.

Although formal and informal groups will exert continuing influence, the administrator is responsible for ensuring that disparities in wealth and influence do not result in a pattern of educational policies that exclude the disaffiliated and relatively anonymous members of the school and community. This is a moral and professional mandate and a necessary condition for long-term stability in the schools. Above all, the administrator must keep in mind that the goal of community power analysis is to develop a sense of community for the school district as a whole.

Procedure for Community Analysis

Community study is a comprehensive activity that will undoubtedly require considerable time and effort on the part of many individuals. It should be part of the administration's plan for public communication. Throughout the analysis procedure, careful filing and recording of information is essential. Here are some positive steps school administrators can take as they piece together the total picture of the community to be served.

Determination of organizational structure.

In addition to structures within the community, reference should also be made to important state agencies and to national organizations that have local chapters. The record should contain both the names of the organizations and a brief indication of their expectations or positions they may have taken previously on educational issues. A sample list might include:
- Government groups—board of education, township and county offices, state board of education, and selected state agencies.
- Volunteer groups—League of Women Voters, NAACP, women's rights, and others.
- Teachers' associations and unions.
- Religious groups, including all numerically significant denominations.
- Business groups—Chamber of Commerce, farm or manufacturing associations, investment bankers' groups.
- Accreditation groups—NCA, NCATE.
- Associations of college teachers and university professors.

Identification of individuals having decision-making roles.

This is a crucial step. In each of the significant groups, the administration should know who the influential personalities are, notwithstanding the formal structure of the organizations involved.

Review of available statistics, records, and documents.

Perusing public and community records can be very helpful in determining the economic, political, and educational trends in a community as well as its values and ideals. Board of education minutes, economic reports, newsletters of local organizations, and membership rosters should be collected, studied, and filed.

Within the school system itself, statistics can reveal the relative success of the school. Comparisons may be made with adjoining districts. Current statistical data pertaining to college admissions, employment success, dropouts, and standardized test scores provide a useful information base in almost any community forum. Of course, as in the study of any organization, statistics can reveal the relative success of the school.

Review of the United States Census.

Census reports provide information relative to sex, race, age, citizenship and place of birth, as well as some more refined breakdowns such as race by sex, age by race, and other combinations. Additionally, information concerning marital status, employment, and income is also found in the reports. Census reports can also serve as a basis for enrollment projection, a critical area of interest to school administrators.

Study of the media and press treatment of the schools.

Town and county newspapers should be read continuously, and relevant articles should be maintained in a scrapbook. The administrator might personally contact newspaper publishers and editors and local radio and TV commentators to discuss identifiable problems and issues. Some determination should be made as to the educational philosophy and expectations of media representatives in order to anticipate their positions on school-related problems.[5]

Study of norms and values.

As indicated previously, the value patterns of most communities are elusive because of the diversity of their various "publics." There are two general approaches that might be adopted in meeting this objective.

First, depending on available time and opportunity, a survey might be developed and distributed. Through random administration of tested survey instruments, statistically valid inferences may be drawn relative to community life (e.g., nature of the home, the place of youth, parent aspirations for their children, general educational levels, acceptance of educational policies and practices). Items in such a survey should be framed in terms of specific questions that the ad-

---

5. Leslie Kindred, *School Personnel Relations* (Englewood Cliffs, N.J.: Prentice Hall, Inc., 1957) pp. 37-40.

ministration feels should be answered. A survey using appropriate sampling techniques to guarantee an acceptable level of statistical confidence, need not be a burdensome and unmanageable task.

Leslie Kindred noted five precautions that should be considered in conducting a survey and in interpreting the results:
- the general nature of the survey should be explained to the community in order to prevent distrust or suspicion;
- printed materials should be examined carefully for bias that may distort the survey findings;
- steps should be taken to prevent the careless use of information by members of the survey staff;
- requests that material be held in confidence should be respected;
- a strictly objective point of view should be maintained in the organization and treatment of survey findings.[6]

The general diagnostic survey is not the only method for assessing community attitudes. Survey instruments can be employed for such purposes as measuring reaction to specific educational or community information programs.

A second approach to discerning value trends is to seek the views of the professional staff in informal interviews or structured workshops. Teachers and guidance counselors are frequently familiar with students' family backgrounds and can render fairly accurate assessments.

Action in the political arena.

It is necessary for the administrator to maintain high visibility in the political community if he is to be functional within it. Among actions that should be taken on a recurring basis are, attendance at relevant legislative sessions, city council meetings, state department of education meetings, and local hearings. Throughout these activities, the administrator should carefully note the input of citizens and politicians for later encounters.

Results of Community Analysis

Because we live in an age of accelerated social change, the status, power structure, and values of the community are in a constant state of flux. Consequently, community analysis is not a process that comes to a logical end, even after prescribed practices have been conducted. As with the entire public communication effort, the self-assurance that is based in certainty will always be wanting. In a very real sense, community analysis can be considered current, but never complete.

Ideally, the analysis of the community and its influence structure will be the cornerstone of the school's communications program. As much as possible, the program should provide the school administrator with reliable information that can be used in decision making. The

6. Ibid., pp. 41-42.

program should indicate the panorama of official organizations and informal groups whose opinions might influence educational matters. It should provide accurate information about the various "publics" that are served by the school district. It should determine action priorities for public communication programs. It should suggest information gaps between the public and the schools. Finally, it should suggest the media and means for communicating with the community.

Issues and Concerns

Conflicts between politicians and educators.

One by-product of the community program is the unavoidable interaction that occurs between politicians and educators. Although both share a sincere interest in community growth and development, a type of competitive rivalry is not unlikely when they are forced to cooperate on the same problems.

One philosophy provides an interesting contrast between the two groups in what it terms their divergent "world views." To the educator, a politician has a "short-term view of the world." He is pragmatic, overly concerned with votes, and quick to compromise for his "political fortunes." Furthermore, the educator sees in the politician an unworkable combination of incomplete information and selective concern for a single ethnic, economic, or sectional interest. The educator also sees a lack of continuity created by the elective process and what educators (and indeed many others) view as the politician's arrogance toward anyone who is not a political equal.

On the other hand, politicians view educators as sanctimonious idealists who founder in generalities and convoluted rhetoric that usually confuses everyone, including themselves. For all their talk of accountability, according to the politician, it is the rare educator who is willing to stand on the results of his efforts.

This thesis is valid inasmuch as both groups tend toward extreme measures in order to accomplish their objectives. We have all heard of the countless educational experiments that are "doomed to success," and of the underhanded politician who will leave the schools in shambles if it means a few votes. Most politicians, of course, are not tricksters; nor are most educators eggheads. The gap can be bridged through patience, hard work, and a realistic understanding of each other's problems and viewpoints.

Differential public influence.

There is a real danger in open meetings that the most vocal and articulate participants will urge their special interests upon the administration. The vast majority may be silent, or more often not even present. Defense of a silent or absent majority can test of the fortitude and resourcefulness of the administration. Facts must be presented straightforwardly, and persuasive opinions must be dealt with in an analytical and, if necessary, critical fashion.

Some community groups are more aggressive than others concerning school policies. Their higher visibility may easily confuse an administrator into overestimating the popular base of a given opinion. In any event, opinions must be respected, but put into proper perspective.

Administrators must develop a healthy and sound regard for the contribution of the professional educator in the community, even when that contribution does not ride the crest of popular assumptions and beliefs. A school system will crack under rigid and autocratic rule, but it will also founder and dissipate when democratic processes run adrift in a morass of self-serving opinions.

The provinciality of community.

In the hands of a weak administrator, the school system can be enveloped by narrow and unenlightened community views that give only the appearance of steady educational progress. However, if communities were fully equipped with educational expertise, there would be no need for school administrators.

Legally, communities control the schools; but administrative leadership is not without influence. School administrators must be assertive, particularly in circumstances where active community groups oppose planned educational change. Although consensus is an important objective, there may be situations where the schools must rise above the community.

Can the Spirit of Community Be Achieved?

Some sociologists and educators have come to view the growing fragmentation of community life as an effect of the social tensions that have pervaded our nation. These people believe that too much is expected of the schools. Schools, they state, are called upon to develop a "humane society" even when the best efforts of our government have failed to achieve economic, social, and racial equality. Since real progress in school-community integration is not possible, why bother trying to achieve it?

The point of this study is that palpable community integration with the schools is both possible and in the best interests of long-term community development. In the first place, "community" and "consensus" are distinct concepts; a spirit of community can be developed even though disagreements exist. The more important condition is that disagreements are channeled through a structure that will guarantee objective and rational consideration of all points of view.

Naturally, the schools can only do their part. Cooperation and commitment are required from other elements in the community as well.

Reporting Information

Burke said that there were three estates in Parliament; but, in the Reporters' Gallery yonder, there sat a Fourth Estate more important far than them all.

—Thomas Carlyle

At an annual college information night at one high school, the principal was forced to delay his opening remarks because the auditorium lighting had to be adjusted. The delay was brief and some 50 or 60 parents who were crowding the corridors quickly filed down the aisles. After some perfunctory overtures to board members in the audience, the principal decided to use the occasion for some remarks about the school district's new program budgeting system. After a clear but lengthy discussion, he introduced two of the school's counselors to continue with the program. First he made polite excuses for the absence of his teaching staff from the conference: "You know, these days of teacher associations and master agreements. . . ."

The counselors' presentation was conducted smoothly. At about 10:15 p.m., the janitors appeared at the side door. One held a broom, the other gazed at the clock—the familiar speaker's cue at the school. The presentation was concluded quickly, and the principal took the microphone for his conventional summary. As usual, he was still asking for questions as the last of the parents exited through the rear door. The presentation ran a bit late, he reflected, but at least all of the information was covered.

The story of college information night at this fictitious school illustrates a major communication problem that can and does occur in real schools throughout the country. There is often a wide margin between what is said and what is heard. Perceived behavior, personality, and appearance have far more impact than any specific information the school administrator may have to convey.

Our hapless principal in our hypothetical situation was obviously attempting to build a castle with dry sand. The parents who attended his meeting may or may not have learned about college opportunities for their youngsters. Surely they learned that planning and communication were not high among the principal's priorities.

The "come what may" attitude has no place in the communications program, given the scarcity of time and the inflated cost of even basic resources. Each aspect of the program must be carefully planned, and a sincere effort must be made to communicate "warmth, interest and concern" to the participants. The communication of feeling, as well as information, should be a guiding principle in the public relations endeavor.[1]

Administrators should consider these minimal ingredients in each interaction with parents and community:
- A significant message that will leave the public with the impression that their time was well spent.
- An orderly presentation of material, in which the most important aspects of the message are emphasized and clearly understood.
- A direct communication where the intellectual and interest level of the community is carefully considered. (Care should be taken to avoid unintentional insults or condescension.)
- Enthusiasm about both the material and those to whom the administrator is communicating.
- Specific, tangible information that the community can think about and remember.

Personal Contact

Few hard and fast rules exist in community relations. But what has been termed the "invitational visitation" technique is almost always more effective than more indirect means of relaying information. Personal contact is time consuming, but in the school system where communication is a priority, it can be achieved with most parents.

Visits by small groups.

A well-publicized policy of open visitation can be useful in encouraging more cooperative interaction between faculty and parents. However, since overly aggressive parents may create an annoyance among staff members, the best approach might be to issue invitations to structured events. For example, administrators might reserve one day each week for a luncheon with selected groups of parents. Parents of new students could be invited to the school for coffee and a brief orientation. Information sessions could also center on specific instructional programs, or on achievements of a particular student group.

Evening visits.

Flexible time arrangements should be created for teachers, counselors, and other personnel to allow for visits at the convenience of

---

1. Richard F. Felicetti, "Are You Communicating Internally?" *NASSP Bulletin*, January 1974, pp. 24-25.

parents. This arrangement is particularly effective for orientation programs and contacts with parents who are new to the school community. Ideally, follow-up printed material should be available at the completion of each of these visits, to reinforce the administrator's message.

Involvement of parents, students, and administrators in extra-curricular activities.

School-sponsored events offer an excellent opportunity for joint participation by adults and adolescents. Faculty sponsors of the various activities should encourage interested adults in the community to participate.

Telephone communications.

The most consistent and justifiable complaint among concerned parents is that telephone inquiries are either put off or forgotten by school personnel. Phone calls should be followed up promptly and courteously. Moreover, personnel should be reminded that for many parents, a phone call is the only means of contact with educational authorities.

School tours.

Tours are best arranged for small groups that share similar interests. They could highlight curricular developments, use of equipment and facilities, or new programs and activities. Film, filmstrips, film cartridges, videotapes, audiotapes, and slides can be useful and effective adjuncts to the school tour.

Speeches

Oratorical skill and executive talent in school administration do not go hand in hand. Unfortunately, however, the overworked public address is an experience that the school administrator can anticipate in almost every phase of his career. Since the prevalent suspicion is that a poor speech is worse than none at all, care must be taken to ensure that successful communication is achieved. The following suggestions can help principals improve their speaking skills.

Preliminary planning.

A minimum of planning is absolutely necessary. No strengths can compensate for the weakness of not knowing a subject well. Similarly, understanding the audience will make it possible to direct the speech to common qualities or interests of the group.

Use of a speaker's booklet.

Excerpts from school policy statements, district goals, educational philosophy, curriculum guides, or other previously successful speeches can be compiled into a booklet. It should be updated periodically with current facts and statistics.

Use of a speech deck.

These cards would contain concise statements or quotes for recurring speeches (such as graduation, career night, back-to-school night). The cards might also refer to journals, books, and other library references that could be consulted for additional information on important topics.

Selective assignment of speakers.

If at all possible, dull or incoherent speakers should not be considered. Often, the presence of a specific staff administrator is not crucial for a given speaking engagement. Although no one will improve without practice, the school community should not be a laboratory for development of speaking skills.

Use of visual aids.

Visual aids are useful for maintaining audience interest and for reinforcing the more significant aspects of the speaker's message. However, they should be employed discreetly to embellish the speaker's central purpose rather than to dominate his delivery.

Written Report Forms

Despite the need to maintain high visibility and personalized communication, administrators are continuously required to report to parents, students, and community in writing. In all written communication, the most elusive variable is "tone," that which the reader infers when he reads "between the lines." Unlike the speaker, the writer cannot repeat for emphasis, explain if misunderstood, or respond immediately to the recipient's initial reaction. Therefore, clarity of message is critical.

School newsletters.

Newsletters should be prepared periodically to inform the public of ongoing school activities. They should be attractive in appearance and friendly and open in style. They should urge personal inquiry regarding points of interest or matters that require clarification.

Program reports.

Too often the results of innovative programs are reserved for administrative councils and boards of education. The assumption that the public lacks the professional or technical acumen necessary for understanding educational programs is both inappropriate and inaccurate. An effort must be made to communicate hard data concerning learning activities in the school. Judicious use of interesting graphs, figures, and other illustrations will attract and maintain reader interest.

School calendar.

A school calendar of important activities and events is helpful in alerting parents to forthcoming events. It should be mailed home during the summer preceding the academic year, or during the first week of school in September.

Organizational handbooks.

Parents and students should have direct access to the written policies, procedures, and regulations that govern the workings of the school. In addition to course offerings, handbooks should describe extracurricular offerings and school policy regarding student rights and responsibilities.

Letters.

Letters constitute the most consistently misused form of written communication with the public. Technical terminology should be paraphrased for the non-specialized reader, and letters should be reviewed for phrases that might convey imprecise meanings or a tone of insincerity and disinterest. Form letters should be avoided unless their use is dictated by constraints of time and finances.

Reporting Through Media

Martin Seiden makes a very critical distinction between two basic attitudes that politicians and public servants are likely to nurture regarding mass media: First, "that the public is malleable because it accepts what it is told." Second, ". . . that it sits in judgment on the information it receives and uses it to form its opinions."[2] The former, more elitist attitude, aims at molding public opinion through artful dissemination of selective information, thereby misleading the public with misrepresented facts.

Though some individuals will be easily persuaded by a one-sided stream of public information, we should not assume that the majority of the public is unaware of the quality of its news stories. Consequently, it is important to emphasize the need for honesty and candor between school officials and representatives of the press, radio, and television.

The media information program is enhanced by preliminary organization and by recognition of several fundamental administrative practices regarding effective communication.

Development of a news and programs calendar.

The calendar could be useful to the principal in organizing information concerning newsworthy events on a chronological basis. For example, the last week in August might feature stories on new courses

---

2. Martin H. Seiden, *Who Controls the Now Media?* (New York: Basic Books, Inc., 1974) p. 64.

and services, beginning teachers, or graduates going to college. The page for September would contain announcements of enrollment figures, anticipated extra class activities and trips, Labor Day programs, and special programs. Later in the year, announcements about commencement, school plays, and concerts could appear along with reports of parent-teacher advisory councils and curriculum committees. The calendar should be extended and modified each year according to changing educational developments and information needs and desires of the community.

Understanding the newsperson's point of view.

The reporter and the educator may often disagree as to what constitutes newsworthy information. Reporters and editors would be hard pressed to publish the large volume of information that is likely to appear in their day-to-day pursuit of relevant and significant news.

According to Fine and Anderson, editors judge information about school or colleges in the context of the following questions:
- Is it timely?
- Is it important?
- Is it newsworthy?
- Is it written in good newspaper style?
- Is it broad?
- Is it of general enough interest?[3]

Use of an "open" school policy.

The open door should apply to newspersons as well as staff and students. Although the open door practice is a constraint on the administrator's time and routine, it is unlikely that the media person will take unfair advantage. Press inquiries about various school system programs should not be hampered by censorship or artificial bureaucratic controls. In fact, all but confidential records should be open to press perusal.

Allowance for timely news releases.

Administrators must recognize that all news is perishable, and that timely dissemination is critical. The news calendar can be a valuable asset in this regard.

Nurturance of a cooperative, productive relationship.

Most important of all is the relationship that is cultivated with media representatives. The administrator's open attitude will be more credible if a deliberate effort is made to keep news personnel informed about school activities and organizational changes. Occasional informal press conferences will allow news people to be more comfortable and candid in the school setting.

---

3. Benjamin Fine and Vivienne Anderson, *The School Administrator and the Press* (New London, Conn.: Arthur C. Croft, 1957).

Conclusion

The information reporting system is a vital aspect of the school administrator's quest for a spirit of community among the publics he serves. A well informed public can act decisively to assist the administration in addressing any range of complex organizational problems. Broader and more serious community participation in school affairs is a valid and predictable outcome of a sound and thorough information program.

It is imperative that the public information program be based on community needs, as manifested by analysis. Openness on the part of administrators cannot be confused with artlessness in the communications effort. Administrators must be careful first to pinpoint their message; second, to select the audience to whom this message should be communicated; third, to select the proper medium for delivery of the message; and finally, to apply communications principles and techniques that are appropriate to the medium and that will achieve the desired effects.

A positive policy of public information is the first, critical step toward more creative methods of active community involvement.

Community Involvement

*'Tis education forms the common mind:
Just as the twig is bent the tree's inclined.*

—Alexander Pope

As with all educational innovations, there is a chance or risk factor when the community relations program progresses beyond mere information sharing to actual community involvement. Certainly, the stakes are high, and mismanaged community involvement is probably worse than none at all. Unplanned or poorly planned community activity can easily lead to mishaps ranging from faculty confusion, poor problem identification, and ineffectual decision making, to frustration and fury on the part of hapless parents and administrators whose expected achievements flounder.

But the prospect of success is worth the risk and the effort, since the possibility for achieving an integrated school-community spirit lies in the balance. For the achievement of "community," good intentions are not enough. Key administrators in the school system must hold consistently to practices that reflect their beliefs and their approach to management.

The first and most basic assumption is a democratic, participatory model of administration that prizes the freedom of each community participant to render opinions on the direction of the educational enterprise. We cannot convince others of the power of individuality and freedom by doubting it ourselves.

Second, if schools are to impart the skills of life, educational managers must understand the impact of change in the twentieth century. The requirements of skill attainment in modern society have gone beyond the capacity of the school specialist. The resources of industry, government, and the community must be tapped. Educators who claim exclusive competence in teaching and learning will restrict and provincialize public education at a time when broad participation is sorely needed.

Finally, those who exercise their right to criticize education should be made to realize their obligation to help fashion the means of improving the circumstances they deplore.[1] Rather than tolerate a nagging critic on the periphery of the school organization, the astute administrator will insist upon responsible participation and constructive thought and action.

Involvement Through Citizen Councils

Advisory groups and citizen councils are often advocated but, unfortunately, are frequently only superficially understood. In the use of such groups, administrative leadership can make the difference between success and failure.

The need for focus.

The purpose of an advisory group must be delineated when the group is formed. This is the first and most essential ingredient of administrative leadership. Individuals "need to know from the beginning just what they are supposed to do, as well as the limits of their participation."[2] Corrections at this juncture are less likely to result in frustration and a loss of confidence.

Individual motivation for council membership is often at variance with the purposes of school administrators. The objective of participation may involve economy, lower taxes, or even censorship of books and instructional materials. For this reason, it must be stated at the outset that the single purpose of involvement is the improvement of the school and its instructional programs. Any other focus of the group is really beyond its purview and is likely to create more problems than it solves.

Council objectives.

The objectives of community councils will vary from district to district, and should be related to needs that are apparent from the community analysis and that are indicated in the communication plan. In general, their efforts may be directed to three areas.

First, community councils can gather and evaluate data in order to clarify district needs and enhance public understanding. Second, they can assist the administration by offering recommendations that will have public respect and confidence. These recommendations will be communicated to others and will be publicized by mass media.[3] Third and most important, the councils' efforts may be instrumental in stimulating a sense of public responsibility for the support and improvement of the schools. By expressing a cross-section of community thought, the groups can become a symbol of a united public will, thereby increasing the likelihood that others will also want to participate in school-related activities.

1. Gordon McCloskey, *Education and Public Understanding* (New York: Harper & Row, 1967) p. 398.
2. C.C. Carpenter, "Principal Leadership and Parent Advisory Groups," *Phi Delta Kappan,* February 1975, p. 426.
3. McCloskey, *Education and Public Understanding,* pp. 412-413.

Cautions.

By carefully considering objectives and maintaining focus, the obvious pitfalls of council activity can be avoided. It is essential in the beginning to secure and maintain full cooperation on the part of the board of education and other members of the administration. They should agree to the goals and potential value of the group.

Rudimentary information sessions for citizen groups are essential. These meetings should clarify the role and responsibility of the board, administration, and faculty. They might also review the legal prerogatives of other elements of the educational organization and speculate on the consequences of infringing on those prerogatives.

Membership.

The most important criterion for membership on a council is a recognition that decision making and fact finding go hand in hand. Decisions cannot be made without hard work. Council members must be willing to devote time to the collection and analysis of data and to participate in the rigorous discussion that is required before a fully informed decision can be rendered.

Persons who have specific informational needs or who are likely to be affected by council decisions and recommendations should be included on the council. In this respect, community analysis is again an extremely useful tool in ensuring that proper contacts have been made and that potentially interested parties have at least been invited to participate.[4]

Group organization.

Sustaining group interaction provides a challenge to the mediation skills of the administrator. The social variables of the group must be considered: age, interests, professional training, and cultural and ethnic backgrounds. Moreover, attention must be given to the normal process of group development and the fact that individual styles of communication normally vary. An effort should be made to assist the less aggressive group member, and to control the glib, dominating leader who might dodge basic issues in order to promote the latest fad.

Generally, the interest and attraction of the group will be maintained only through administrative leadership and organization. The administrator's task with any council is to guide interaction through three basic levels of development. In the *involvement level*, individual and group purposes are clarified. It is important at this state that individuals become comfortable with each other and that a trusting relationship is established.

Once a team spirit has been formed in the council, the *working level* is entered. At this level, the group considers alternatives to spec-

---

4. William J. Banoch and Richard H. Escott, "The Public as a Problem: What to Do?" *School Management*, March 1973, pp. 32-33.

ified problems it must solve. It is essential at this level that each individual recognize his own predilections regarding basic problems and consent to examine data and derive conclusions independently.

Since the council is established to study specific problems, it is only logical that it result in definitive recommendations for school policy or practice. At the *recommendation stage*, the group should prepare its conclusions and ensure that they have a factual foundation and the representation of the entire group. These recommendations should be shared with school authorities and released to the general public.

Group development.

It is the administrator's responsibility to guide the group through the working level and increase the motivation and capacity of members for effective interaction and problem solving. The administrator is an energizer; he prods, stimulates, and arouses greater activity and a higher quality of individual and group performance.[5]

The following are ways in which the school administrator can effect greater group productivity:
- By aggressively seeking and providing information, offering authoritative facts and generalizations, clarifying values;
- By elaborating—spelling out suggestions, and providing illustrations;
- By coordinating—synthesizing group opinion, pointing out the relationships among ideas and suggestions;
- By assisting with group procedures, expediting performance of routine tasks such as recording and distributing materials;
- By supporting individual participation—increasing solidarity by praising and showing interest in the contribution of each group member;
- By setting standards, constantly examining the quality of ideas against standards such as logic, practicality, utility, and relevance;
- By managing conflict, taking necessary steps to ensure that the group does not become stymied by meaningless argument.

Involvement of Volunteers

The potential value of a volunteer program cannot be overlooked by a school administrator who is interested in expanding the school's public communication base. The volunteer program is more than a channel to the community; it can also release teachers from nonteaching chores, enabling them to assist in seeking new and creative learning structures.

The activities of volunteers are limited only by their own efforts and the willingness of administrators to experiment and capitalize on

---

5. Rensis Likert, *New Patterns of Management* (New York: McGraw Hill, 1961) pp. 162-170.

their abilities and interests. Clerical tasks such as typing, correcting papers, and maintaining attendance records are typical volunteer activities.

However, a more active role for the volunteer worker has been implemented in some school districts. Individuals with specialized skills in foreign languages, math, or science are encouraged to work with students on an individual, tutorial basis. Others, with nursing or paraprofessional medical experience, can be of great value to the school health staff. Because of their familiarity with community resources, volunteers can also be enthusiastic project planners for educational trips and extended student field work.

The New Providence school district in New Jersey has piloted a well-organized model entitled the Volunteer Aide Program. A part-time project aide leader is responsible for establishing qualifications, inventorying individual skills, interviewing, and assigning responsibilities. The program is enhanced by structured orientation activities and evaluation.[6]

To achieve optimal success from a volunteer program, administrators should consider the following guidelines:

- A project director should plan volunteer activity around specific school needs. Duplication of effort should be avoided.
- Allocation of tasks should be commensurate with individual ability. Care must be exercised to ensure that aides are not given responsibilities that are beyond their level of competence.
- Volunteers should be given full and proper orientation, especially when their responsibilities involve the management of students.
- The contribution of volunteers should be recognized through school media and in official administrative and board meetings.
- Professional time saved as a result of volunteer activities should be used wisely.

Curriculum Experience in the Community

For too long in public education, the community experience has been an adjunct rather than a vital, integrated aspect of total student learning. For too long we have used a tiny lens in estimating school-community possibilities, and the result has been a narrow focus. Consider the limitations of industrial or business education that takes place only within the walls of school buildings. The weight of tradition is heavy, and it can only be eased by imagination and assertiveness on the part of educational administrators.

The value of integrating the community and educational experience has been recognized for some time. In 1963, James Jones recommended more active utilization of community institutions, services, and processes with a wide range of objectives to include "vocational,

---

6. Edward M. Schmidt, "The Volunteer Aide Program in New Providence," *The Administrator Quarterly*, Spring 1975, pp. 10-12.

social, citizenship, leisure, cultural, agricultural, health and guidance."[7]

The stumbling block in recent years seems to be that educators have applied more rhetoric than action to the potential role of community in enhancing the curriculum. The key step is recognition of one basic, operative principle: that the community should be considered an extension of the curriculum, a basic element in the same sense as classrooms, books, and other instructional resources.

Model programs.

Significant gains have been made in the last decade in business and career education. This is because administrators and teachers have carefully highlighted program objectives and matched community resources to student needs. Consequently, on-the-job training, cooperative work experience, and other career education projects have developed and thrived.

The example of career education has been emulated in the development of other highly creative educational experiences with considerable potential for firming the bond between school and community. One example is the Yosemite Park Institute, which was created for high school students and faculty interested in ecology. The Yosemite staff consists of park employees and leaders from the Carey Company, a group of government, academic, and business professionals. The Institute provides one-week seminars on various environmental issues. During regular school time, students are given "stimulating educational experiences directed toward improvement of environmental programs and ethics." When they return to the high school, students share their experiences with the general student body.[8]

Another innovative school-community cooperative program was recently undertaken by the Cinnaminson (N.J.) School District under the aegis of the Executive High School Internship Program, based in New York City. The Executive Internship Program enables high school juniors and seniors to spend a full semester with a senior official in government, an educational or cultural institution, a private civic agency, an agency providing direct services to community residents, or some other organization with broad public interest. Executive Interns work with judges, commissioners, administrators of government agencies, business executives, television producers and directors, newspaper and magazine editors, hospital administrators, and museum curators.

The Executive Internship Program is broadly educational. It introduces students to the ways that executives and managers function as decision makers in an organizational setting. In addition, students learn how they themselves can function effectively in an organiza-

7. James J. Jones, *School Public Relations* (New York: Center for Applied Research, Inc., 1966) pp. 27-28.

8. Franklin J. Thompson, "Developing Programs Around Out of School Experiences," *NASSP Bulletin*, May 1974, pp. 174-75.

tion. Interns refine their social and intellectual skills by relating to a variety of adults, writing reports, becoming precise in their analyses of policy issues, organizing community-based programs, and actively initiating their own learning experiences. They gain specific knowledge about budget, personnel administration, organizational development, program planning and implementation, delivery of services to clients, and the assessment of program results and policies.

In the process, Executive Interns can also explore possible career options and help to serve the community. They become valuable resources to their high schools because of their first-hand knowledge about policy development, management, service delivery, and the world of employment. Through their many contacts, Interns can help teachers and administrators relate to various government agencies and organizations and understand private industry.[9]

Some of the most creative community-based educational projects were reported by the National Association of Secondary School Principals' Wingspread Conference in 1974. Project Impact, set in the small, rural town of Hoffman, Minn., aims to enhance student understanding of community institutions and encourage them to give of themselves by assisting younger children and mentally retarded adults. Approximately 60 students participate directly in tutoring, teaching, and visiting in an elementary school, a home for retarded adults, and a nursing home. They are supervised by regular and special education staff, and their experiences are reinforced once they have returned to their classroom.[10]

In Lansing, Mich., efforts are being undertaken on a regional level to provide accredited learning experiences in the community at large. A health careers exploration program provides students from several area high schools with lectures and seminars "featuring doctors, nurses, hospital administrators, etc." One high school in the city has teamed up with other schools "to offer a program in metropolitan studies which has students from both districts working on site with government agencies, social service groups and so on."[11]

Program characteristics.

It is apparent from the preceding discussion that there has not yet developed a single, acceptable definition of the community-based curriculum. The scope and objectives of the programs are limited only by the imagination of those who initiate and implement them. Nevertheless, the programs have characteristic features that reflect sound educational principles:
- Community-based programs normally involve a substantial de-

---

9 Lee Oberporleiter and Robert Byrne, *Executive High School Internship* (Cinnaminson, N.J.: Cinnaminson Township Public Schools, 1975).

10. Margaret Herinksen and Richard A. Parks, "Mutually Beneficial Cooperation," *NASSP Bulletin*, November 1974, pp. 29-32.

11. Gerald E. Kasler, "Relations With The Community in Action Learning Programs," *NASSP Bulletin*, November 1974, pp. 48-49.

gree of independent study, wherein the learning activity is largely motivated by the learner's own aims and rewarded in terms of its intrinsic values.
- The programs represent a break from traditional secondary school instructional practices in utilizing the services of teachers and other professionals primarily as resources for the learner.
- The programs are mainly "quest type." They emphasize exploration, extension, and refinement of student aptitudes and interests that may or may not be related to career choices.
- The programs provide a unique opportunity for student appreciation and appraisal of the communities that the schools serve.
- The learning experiences result in critical and analytical independent thinking that is focused on real world problems and issues.

Administrative considerations.

For the administrator of a community-based curriculum a high level of coordination, leadership, and management skill is required.
- Faculty and administration will need to cooperate in the identification of community learning sites. Liaison and communication become increasingly important.
- Staff development through workshops, sensitivity sessions, and general inservice training is required in order to motivate teachers to implement community-based projects.
- Staff selection must account for community awareness and greater interpersonal skill among potential teachers.
- Pupil evaluation procedures must be revamped to account for these action-learning activities. Methods should be devised for granting full or partial credit for learning accomplished in the community.

Increasing Parent Involvement

The burden of parent-school interaction is invariably shouldered by an enthusiastic but shrinking group of parents and educators. Increased parental pressure in the schools depends on an accurate diagnosis of those adults who prefer to be uninvolved in the learning of their children. The School Management Institute of Westerville, Ohio, has developed a theoretical framework that suggests four types of parents who traditionally remain aloof from school life: the apathetic, the hostile, the shy, and the preoccupied.

To the apathetic parent, the child's life in school is relatively unimportant. The responsibilities of schooling and parenthood are viewed as separate and distinct. In attracting this group to the school, it is necessary for educators to meet the parents on their own terms by responding to their interests and needs. Through social functions and special interest classes, the parents may become familiar with the school, its personnel, and its educational program.

Hostile parents are self-appointed critics who denounce school programs on the basis of selective information. Such parents require a forum for expression of their views. Group interaction with trained administrators and counselors can lead to more improved communication through understanding.

Such a program was recently conducted in the Sewanhaka school district on Long Island. Parents were offered group counseling to sensitize them to the complexities of adolescent development, so that positive action could be taken to assist the youngsters in their academic and social progress.[12] A sequential program was planned involving discussion topics such as the teenager and his social surroundings, the teenager's view of himself, the effect of authority, competition, and rejection, and methods of reinforcing positive self-image among young people. The program was successful as a planned intervention technique involving home and school in meeting specific needs in the areas of socialization, discipline, and achievement.

The shy and preoccupied parents are perhaps the most difficult to deal with. Shy parents avoid the school because of an anticipated feeling of discomfort. They may want to know more, but they are afraid to ask. Preoccupied parents are more concerned with their own problems and circumstances. For these parents, mere invitations are not enough. The school must be made to be a vital place, and involvement must be rewarded.

Several strategies have been found successful in increasing parental involvement. First, there is no better motivation than the home visit; parents are then not only invited, but led to the schoolhouse door. When a home visit is impossible, the school district can be separated into zones of responsibility for given groups of administrators, counselors, or teachers. Visits are then made to community centers, local stores, and churches in order to seek the parents in their own environment. In the case of parents who are preoccupied with their own circumstances, school personnel may be able to offer both empathy and assistance. Under the best conditions, the parents will view the educators as allies, and reciprocate by visiting and helping the school.

Conclusion

School-community relationships can be analyzed according to four basic views, ranging from a highly traditional separation of school and community to a more creative model of united activity and purpose.

The first view separates the function of the school and community entirely. The former is for learning, the latter for living. A second view allows for a degree of overlap, although there is a basic belief that the curriculum need not coincide with the community and its

---

12. Robert Byrne, "Parent Group Interaction—An Application of Title I Funds," *The Guidance Clinic*, January 1975, pp. 12-14.

aspirations. Both of these views are conventional and conservative, and allow for minimal and selective communication between the school and the taxpayers it serves.

According to the third view, the school is a small circle within a larger community circle. It is responsible to the community and facilitates its objectives through educational programs. Finally, in the school of the future, the small circle breaks out to the point where it is impossible to determine where the community and school begin and end. The school becomes a community building, an education center wherein all people are both teachers and learners.

Hopefully, this type of community school, involving total integration of programs and services, will be the model of educational excellence for the second half of the twentieth century. Then the quest for unified school-community action and the spirit of community will have been achieved.

About the authors. Robert Byrne is principal of Cinnaminson High School, Cinnaminson, N.J. Edward Powell is superintendent of schools in Dover, Del.